AEROSPACE ENGINEER

APRILLE ERICSSON

LAURA HAMILTON WAXMAN

Lerner Publications

The publisher wishes to thank Aprille Ericsson for providing some of the photos that appear in this book.

Lerner Publications Company
A division of Lerner Publishing Group, Inc.
241 First Avenue North
Minneapolis, MN 55401 USA

For reading levels and more information, look up this title at www.lernerbooks.com.

Content Consultant: John Weyrauch, Industrial Professor of Design, Aerospace Engineering and Mechanics, University of Minnesota

Library of Congress Cataloging-in-Publication Data

Waxman, Laura Hamilton.
    Aerospace engineer Aprille Ericsson / by Laura Hamilton Waxman.
        pages   cm. — (STEM trailblazer bios)
    Includes bibliographical references and index.
    ISBN 978-1-4677-5793-5 (lib. bdg. : alk. paper)
    ISBN 978-1-4677-6282-3 (eBook)
    1. Ericsson, Aprille, 1963– 2. Aerospace engineers—United States—Biography—Juvenile literature. 3. African American women aerospace engineers—United States—Biography—Juvenile literature. I. Title.
    TL540.E633W39 2015
    629.4092—dc23 [B]   2014013767

Manufactured in the United States of America
1 – PC – 12/31/14

The images in this book are used with the permission of: © Carlos Davila/Photographer's Choice/ Getty Images, p. 4; Courtesy of Aprille Ericsson, pp. 5, 8, 13, 20, 24; NASA/JSC PAO Web Team, p. 7; © iStockphoto.com/DenisTangneyJr, p. 9; © OSHIKAZU TSUNO/AFP/Getty Images, p. 10; © iStockphoto.com/rabbit75_ist, p. 11; © Bettmann/CORBIS, p. 15; NASA/JSC PAO Web Team, p. 16; © Angus Osborn/Dorling Kindersley/Getty Images, p. 17; NASA/Goddard Space Flight Center, p. 18; NASA/Goddard/MIT/Brown, p. 21; NASA/Dana Berry/Skyworks Digital, p. 22; NASA, p. 25; © Elena Olivo, p. 26.

Front cover: Courtesy of Aprille Ericsson.

Main body text set in Adrianna Regular 13/22. Typeface provided by Chank.

CONTENTS

Chapter 1

Landing on the moon was a distant dream in the early 1960s.

DREAMING
BIG

In 1961, President John F. Kennedy made a bold promise. He said that the United States would send an American to the moon in the next decade. To some people, President Kennedy seemed like a dreamer. They doubted that such an ambitious goal could ever really be within reach.

Another dreamer was born two years later on April 1, 1963. Her name was Aprille Joy Ericsson. Aprille grew up in a poor neighborhood in Brooklyn, New York. She lived with her mom and two younger sisters in public housing. The government provided this housing at a low rent.

Aprille's family may not have had a lot of money, but they had plenty of love. Aprille had big dreams for her life, and her family supported her in everything she did.

Aprille plays at the beach in 1967.

One of Aprille's dreams was to be an astronaut. In first grade, she watched something amazing on TV. US astronauts Neil Armstrong, Buzz Aldrin, and Michael Collins traveled to the moon on *Apollo 11*. Seeing Kennedy's dream come true inspired Aprille. She wondered if maybe she could help out on future space missions. But Aprille had other dreams too, such as being an artist, a lawyer, or maybe even a track star!

SPACE RACE

During Aprille's childhood, the United States was involved in an unofficial competition known as the Space Race. It started in 1957 when the Soviet Union (fifteen republics that included Russia) launched the first spacecraft. Americans saw the Soviets as their greatest competitors. In 1958, the United States created NASA, the National Aeronautics and Space Administration. NASA's goal was to not only keep up with the Soviets but to surpass them.

Buzz Aldrin poses next to the American flag on the surface of the moon on July 20, 1969.

TURNING TO MATH AND SCIENCE

In middle school, Aprille fell in love with math and science. This budding interest made her feel different from her peers. Not many other girls or African Americans in her school had a passion for those subjects. But that didn't stop Aprille. She became the only African American to be placed in advanced classes in her school's Special Progress program. She also won second place in the school's science fair.

Aprille worked hard in school, but she wasn't just a good student. She pursued interests outside the classroom too. She played basketball, did gymnastics, and loved performing with her school's band.

Aprille enjoys playing softball in her free time. Here she waits for a pitch during a game in 1996.

Aprille moved to Cambridge, Massachusetts, to attend high school.

After middle school, Aprille had a big choice to make. She had been accepted to some of the city's top public high schools. She also got a scholarship to attend a private school in Cambridge, Massachusetts, where her grandparents lived. At the age of fifteen, she decided to live with her grandparents so that she could attend the private school. It wouldn't be easy, but she knew she could do it.

Chapter 2

Simulators help pilots and astronauts train for flights. These machines are also used to test new aircraft designs.

WORKING
HARD

Aprille studied hard at her new school. She became a top student and continued to be involved in extracurricular activities. But she still wasn't sure what she wanted to do with her life.

That started to change the summer after eleventh grade. Aprille took part in a special program run by the Massachusetts Institute of Technology (MIT). The program was for talented minority students interested in **engineering**. Aprille got to visit an air force base, where she used a **flight simulator** and watched planes from inside a control tower. That experience renewed her passion for a career in **aerospace**.

Massachusetts Institute of Technology (MIT) is one of the top colleges for science and engineering.

TECH TALK

"Entering high-tech fields such as science, engineering, and technology is tough by any standards. . . . But it's especially challenging for females. . . . They often have very few role models in these careers and are not strongly encouraged to enter such fields as young girls."

—*Aprille Ericsson*

STUDYING AEROSPACE ENGINEERING

Ericsson graduated from high school with top honors. She enrolled in college at MIT to study engineering for air and space travel. That meant learning how to build and operate tools and machines for space. At MIT, Ericsson worked on projects for human spaceflight. She helped invent instruments to use in space. She even studied and made a plan for how a vehicle could explore Mars. These projects only strengthened her desire to become an aerospace engineer.

At the time, very few women or African Americans were aerospace engineers. Ericsson would have to work hard to make her dream come true. But hard work never stopped Ericsson. She spent many late nights studying. Sometimes it was challenging to keep her eyes open. To get inspired, she would look at a poster on her wall that her mom and one of her sisters gave her. It showed great African American women from the past, such as Sojourner Truth and Harriet Tubman. These women had made a difference by being brave and working hard. Thinking about them kept Ericsson going.

Ericsson accepts her diploma from MIT in 1986.

A NEW CHALLENGE

Ericsson graduated from MIT in 1986. She wanted to work for NASA, but disaster had struck four months earlier. A NASA spacecraft called *Challenger* had exploded just after takeoff, and all seven astronauts inside had died. Americans suddenly felt a bit tentative about the space program. The US government began to invest more resources in a different, non-space-related project—making missiles. That work would require engineers such as Ericsson, but Ericsson wasn't interested in creating weapons. She wanted to help humans explore outer space. Somehow, she knew she would find a way to make her dreams a reality.

TECH TALK

"If I'm a 'giant in science,' it is only because I stand on the shoulders of my forefathers. We must go back and reclaim our past so we can move forward."

—*Aprille Ericsson*

The space shuttle *Challenger* exploded shortly after takeoff on January 28, 1986.

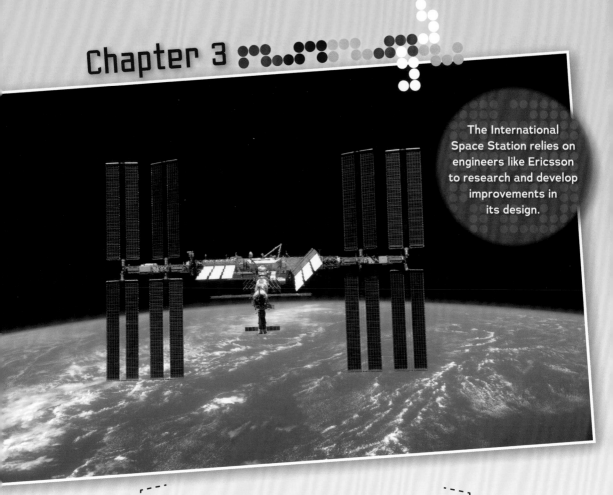

Chapter 3

The International Space Station relies on engineers like Ericsson to research and develop improvements in its design.

CHASING
THE DREAM

Ericsson had faced many challenges in her life. She hadn't given up in the past, and she wasn't about to give up this time. Instead, she came up with a new plan. She decided to go back to school to study at the Large Space Structures

Institute at Howard University. There she learned to solve problems for large space structures, such as the International Space Station.

MAKING IT COME TRUE

Ericsson's work at Howard University took her all around the world. She shared her ideas in countries such as Germany, Canada, and England. While at Howard, something else important happened. In 1992, she got a job at NASA with the

A friend encouraged Ericsson to enroll at Howard University for graduate school.

Goddard Space Flight Center (GSFC) in Maryland. She began working there as an aerospace engineer while still going to school.

Three years later, Ericsson earned a PhD in mechanical engineering, aerospace option. She became the first African American woman to achieve that goal at Howard University. She also became the first African American woman at GSFC to earn a PhD in engineering.

Goddard Space Flight Center builds and monitors spacecraft, like the Hubble Space Telescope.

TECH TALK

"I didn't start out to be the first African American female to receive a PhD in mechanical engineering, the Aerospace Option, from Howard University. . . . But I am proud to be, and I try to represent well for all others that come behind me."

—*Aprille Ericsson*

Ericsson had worked hard, and she hadn't given up. She was finally an engineer at NASA. But she had more dreams to pursue. She hoped to work on many exciting NASA missions in the future.

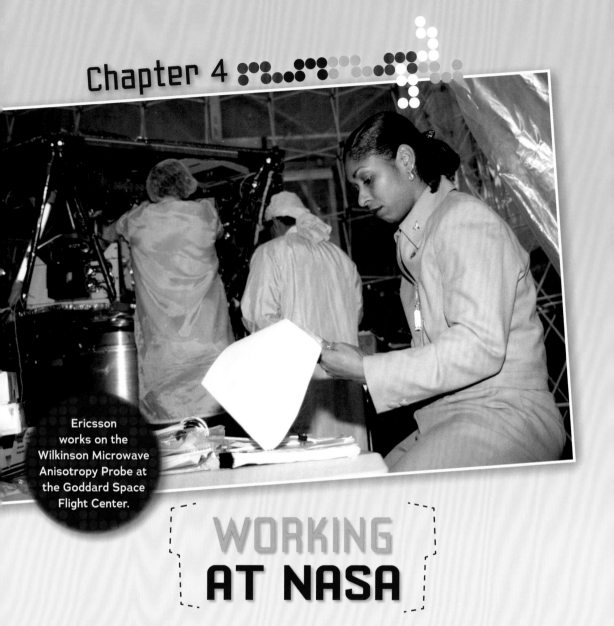

Chapter 4

Ericsson works on the Wilkinson Microwave Anisotropy Probe at the Goddard Space Flight Center.

WORKING AT NASA

Ericsson spent most of her career at NASA, and that is where she still works. Through the years, she has worked on many different missions and led many teams of NASA engineers and other workers. She goes wherever she is needed most. One of her main responsibilities as an aerospace engineer has been to make sure that the instruments on NASA's spacecraft work properly. Many of these spacecraft are different types of **satellites**.

WORKING ON SPACE MISSIONS

Ericsson's work has helped scientists learn more about the moon and outer space. For example, she worked on the Lunar Orbiter Laser Altimeter (LOLA) mission. For LOLA, she designed and tested instruments to help make a new map of the moon for future astronauts. For another project, she designed and developed missions for bringing soil and rocks from Mars back to Earth for further study.

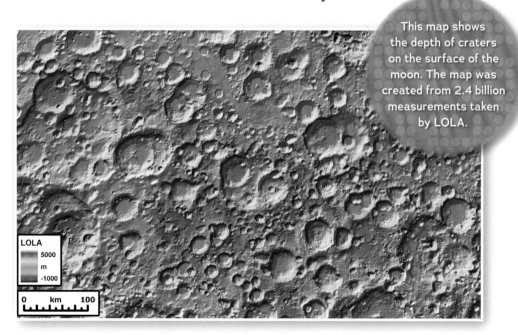

This map shows the depth of craters on the surface of the moon. The map was created from 2.4 billion measurements taken by LOLA.

LOLA

5000
m
-1000

0   km   100

Ericsson has also worked on many satellites that explored deep space. One such satellite was called the Rossi X-ray Timing Explorer (RXTE). The RXTE measured the X-rays coming from deep space objects, such as dying stars and **black holes**. That information has helped improve scientists' understanding of distant objects in space. Another satellite Ericsson worked on was the Wilkinson Microwave Anisotropy Probe (WMAP). WMAP collected temperature data that helped scientists try to determine the age of the universe. Scientists also hope to learn how the universe has changed over time. Ericsson's work is helping them find answers to these complicated questions.

The Rossi X-ray Timing Explorer is used to study the X-rays given off by black holes.

TECH TALK

"At NASA we are doing incredible scientific research and we are making an investment in our future. . . . It makes me feel good to know that my work has real-life implications."

—*Aprille Ericsson*

HELPING OUR PLANET

Ericsson has helped scientists learn about our changing planet too. Certain gases in Earth's atmosphere, known as greenhouse gases, are affecting our planet's climate. Ericsson has worked on projects to measure how greenhouse gases are changing our weather.

One project, called the Tropical Rainfall Measuring Mission, used a satellite to measure how much rain falls in tropical parts of the world. This satellite has helped scientists predict how Earth's weather might change in the future. It also helps them understand how big the problem of greenhouse gases might be for our planet.

Ericsson works with sensitive satellites that need protection from dust and dirt. She uses a special lab called the High Bay Clean Room to protect these machines.

One of Ericsson's most recent projects will help scientists to study Earth's **polar ice caps**. Greenhouse gases are warming the North and South Poles. The warmer temperatures are causing the ice caps to melt slowly. Scientists will soon be able to find out more with the new Ice, Cloud, and Land Elevation Satellite (ICESat-2). Ericsson was one of the managers in charge of creating a large instrument for ICESat-2 called ATLAS (Advanced Topographic Laser Altimeter System). The device will be attached to ICESat-2 and will use lasers to measure the size of the ice caps. ICESat-2 is scheduled to launch in 2016.

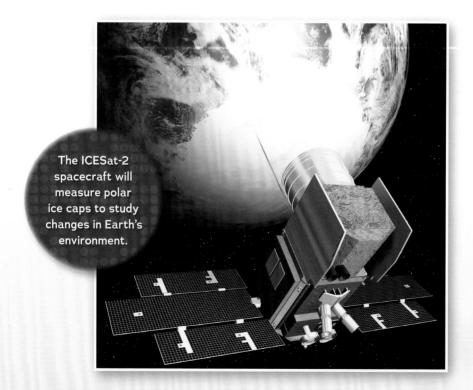

The ICESat-2 spacecraft will measure polar ice caps to study changes in Earth's environment.

Chapter 5

Ericsson speaks with students at the Women's Summit at Polytechnic Institute of New York University in March 2013.

SHARING
THE DREAM

Ericsson has won dozens of awards and honors for her work at NASA. One of her biggest honors was winning the Women in Science and Engineering Award. She received this award for being the best female engineer in the federal

government. She's also been named a Giant in Science and a Science Trailblazer and has been listed as one of the Top 50 Minority Women in Science and Engineering.

INSPIRING OTHERS

Ericsson is using her fame as a scientist to help others. She believes more girls and people of color should become scientists. She works with students of all ages to show them the excitement of working in math and science.

Ericsson also gives many encouraging speeches to students. She has even been invited to speak to students at

Ericsson (left) gives advice on how students can prepare for STEM (Science, Technology, Engineering, and Math) careers during a NASA webcast with students and teachers in February 2012.

the White House. She tells young people to "read, read, read, and learn, learn, learn," and to work hard, shoot for the moon, and follow their dreams.

Ericsson continues to inspire others with her work every day. No matter what new project she is tackling, she always works hard and does her best.

TECH TALK

"Being smart and committed to learning new things has had its rewards. I have been to the White House several times. I have been able to present my research and speak around the United States, Canada, Germany, and England. . . . I've even attended a space shuttle launch. So remember that it's okay to be an intelligent woman."

—Aprille Ericsson

TIMELINE

1963

Aprille Joy Ericsson is born in Brooklyn, New York, on April 1.

1986

Ericsson graduates from MIT with a bachelor of science degree in aeronautical/astronautical engineering, four months after the *Challenger* disaster.

1992

Ericsson gets a job at NASA's Goddard Space Flight Center in Maryland.

1995

Ericsson becomes the first woman to earn a PhD in mechanical engineering from Howard University.

1997

Ericsson receives the Women in Science and Engineering Award, one of many awards she will earn.

2009

The Lunar Orbiter Laser Altimeter (LOLA), which Ericsson worked on, launches.

2010

Ericsson speaks at the White House as part of First Lady Michelle Obama's mentoring program for high school girls.

2013

Ericsson serves as an international speaker for the Women in Engineering Conference in South Africa for the third consecutive year.

SOURCE NOTES

12 "Female Aerospace Engineer from NASA Addresses GEM-SET Event at UCSD to Encourage More Girls in Science," *La Prensa San Diego Bilingual Newspaper*, 2003, accessed April 11, 2014, http://www.laprensa-sandiego.org/archieve/april04-03/gemset.htm

14 Audrey Fischer, "'Read, Read, Read—Learn, Learn, Learn': Aprille Ericsson-Jackson Opens Women's History Month," *Library of Congress Information Bulletin*, 2001, accessed April 11, 2014, http://www.loc.gov/loc/lcib/0104/rocketeer.html

19 Karen Asher, "Aprille Ericsson-Jackson, Ph.D.," *UVA NewsMakers*, 2003, accessed April 11, 2014, http://www.virginia.edu/uvanewsmakers/newsmakers/ericsson-jackson.html

23 Ibid.

28 Fischer, "'Read, Read, Read—Learn, Learn, Learn.'"

28 Asher, "Aprille Ericsson-Jackson, Ph.D."

GLOSSARY

aerospace
the design or operation of spacecraft

black holes
invisible objects in space that pull everything into them, including light

engineering
the science of designing and building

flight simulator
a machine that imitates the controls of an airplane or a spacecraft

polar ice caps
large, thick sheets of ice at the North and South Poles

satellites
objects that circle planets, moons, or stars in space

FURTHER INFORMATION

BOOKS

Doeden, Matt. *SpaceX and Tesla Motors Engineer Elon Musk*. Minneapolis: Lerner Publications, 2015. Will humans ever live on another planet? Learn about the engineer who's trying to make it happen.

Ventura, Marne. *Astrophysicist and Space Advocate Neil deGrasse Tyson*. Minneapolis: Lerner Publications, 2014. Love outer space? Find out how Neil deGrasse Tyson went from starstruck kid to popular space expert.

Waxman, Laura Hamilton. *Exploring Space Travel*. Minneapolis: Lerner Publications, 2012. Discover what it takes to get into outer space and what being in space is like for astronauts.

WEBSITES

Goddard Space Flight Center
http://www.nasa.gov/centers/goddard/home/index.html
Learn more about the place where Ericsson has spent her career.

NASA Women of STEM
http://www.nasa.gov/education/womenstem/#.Uyc7H4X6-FU
Discover how women such as Ericsson are using math and science in their jobs at NASA.

Science for Kids
http://kids.usa.gov/science/index.shtml
Check out this site to get science fair project ideas, learn about scientists and inventors, and explore science-related jobs.

LERNER
SOURCE

Expand learning beyond the printed book. Download free, complementary educational resources for this book from our website, www.lernerresource.com.

INDEX

ABOUT THE AUTHOR

Laura Hamilton Waxman has written many nonfiction books for young readers. She particularly enjoys writing about people such as Aprille Ericsson who have shaped our world.

B
ERI

Waxman, Laura
  Hamilton.

Aerospace engineer
Aprille Ericsson.

30061000471967

$26.65

DATE			
		NOV 18 2016	

003441   9640728